This Log Book belong(s to)
Capt. _____

Do you want to easily keep track of all of the places you have visited: past, present, and future?

This log book is the answer! In its pages is a set of 50 state maps, each showing county boundaries, major cities, and interstate highways. You can also enter *log notes* documenting highlights of your trips. Checklists of Countries of the World and US National Parks are also included in the book.

Make vibrant state maps showing your travels, using colored pencils to shade in the counties you have visited. A road atlas is recommended as a reference for charting your journeys. Reminisce with family and friends as you reconstruct the routes of prior trips you have taken.

Every member of the family will want a log book! You can also obtain a FREE county checklist from *Personalized Map Company's* web site (**www.mymaps.com**). Directions are included to make a national map of your counties on your computer monitor.

May you have many memorable adventures!

My Own Captain's Log Book, 4th edition
Copyright © 2022 Personalized Map Company | www.mymaps.com

Alabama

Log Notes:

Alaska

Log Notes: _____

Arizona

Log Notes:

Arkansas

Log Notes:

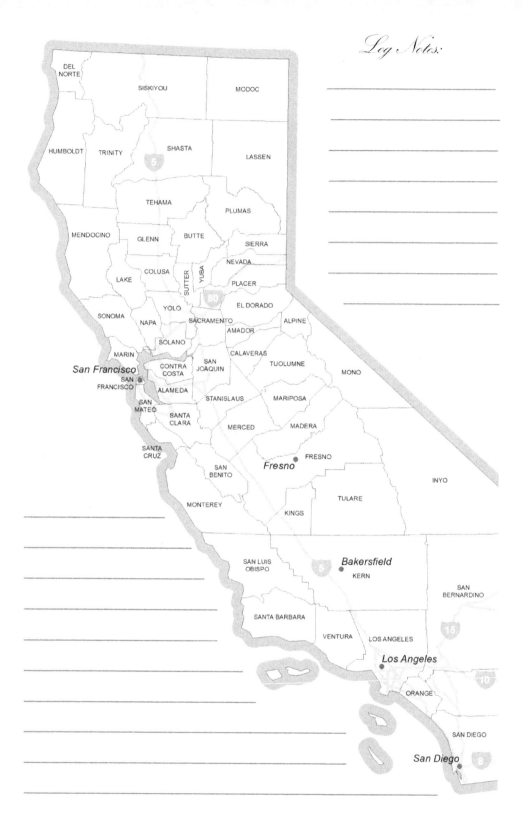

California

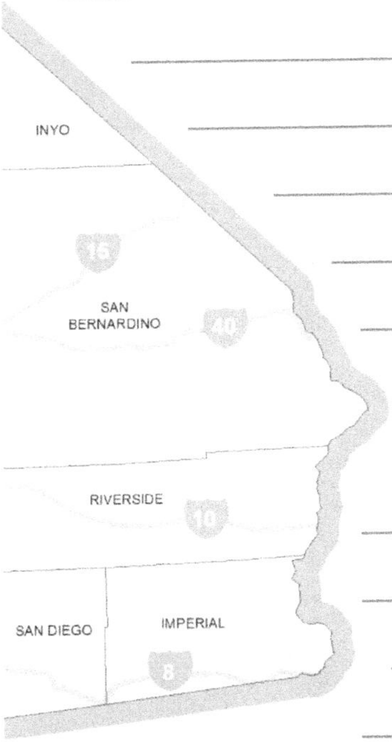

Colorado

Log Notes:

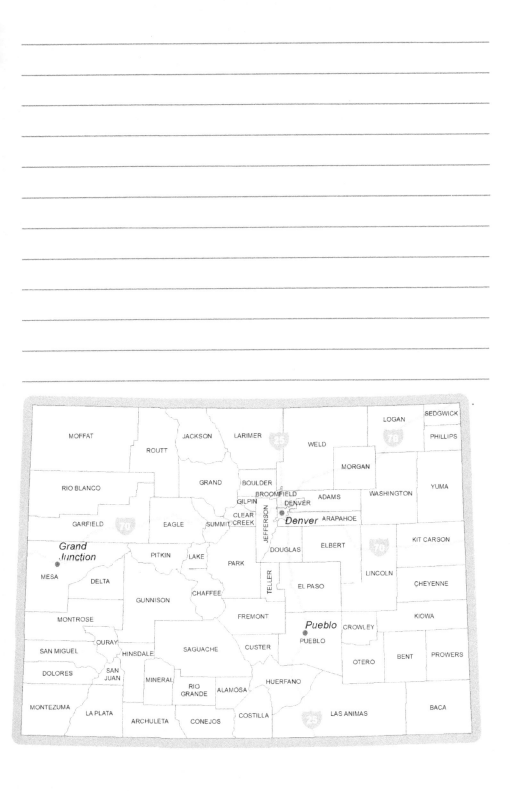

Connecticut

Log Notes:

Delaware

Log Notes: _____

_____
_____
_____
_____
_____
_____
_____
_____
_____
_____
_____
_____
_____

District of Columbia

Log Notes: _____

_____
_____
_____
_____
_____
_____
_____
_____
_____
_____
_____

Florida

Log Notes:

Georgia

Log Notes:

Hawaii

Log Notes:

Idaho

Log Notes: _____

_____

_____

_____

_____

_____

_____

_____

_____

_____

_____

_____

Illinois

Log Notes:

Indiana

Log Notes:

Iowa

Log Notes:

Kansas

Log Notes:

Kentucky

Log Notes:

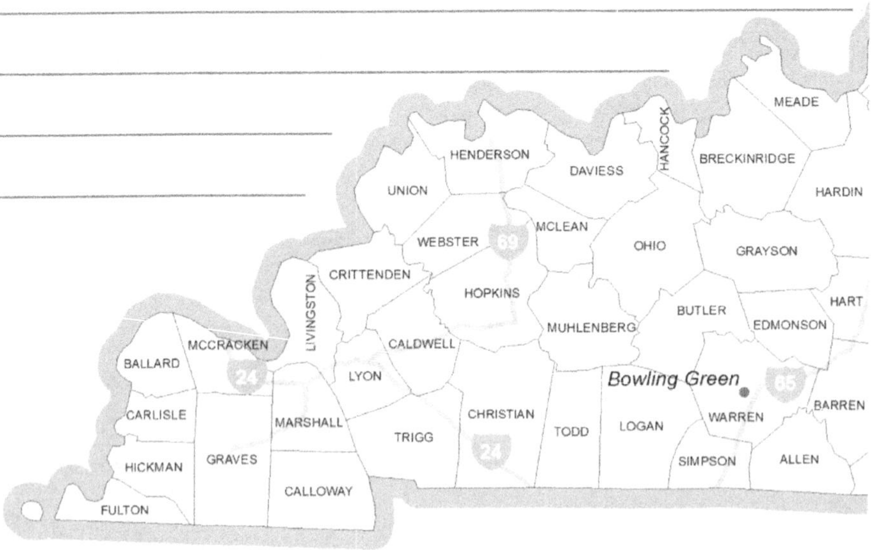

Louisiana

Log Notes: _____

Maine

Log Notes:

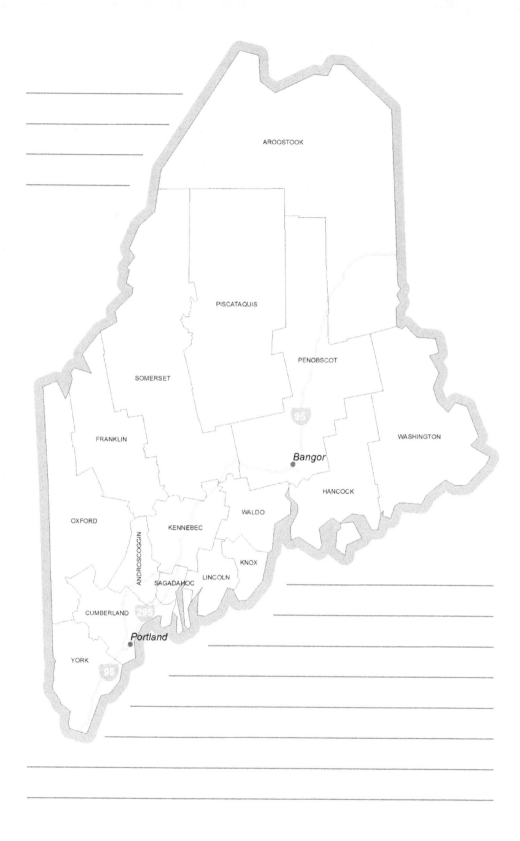

Maryland

Log Notes:

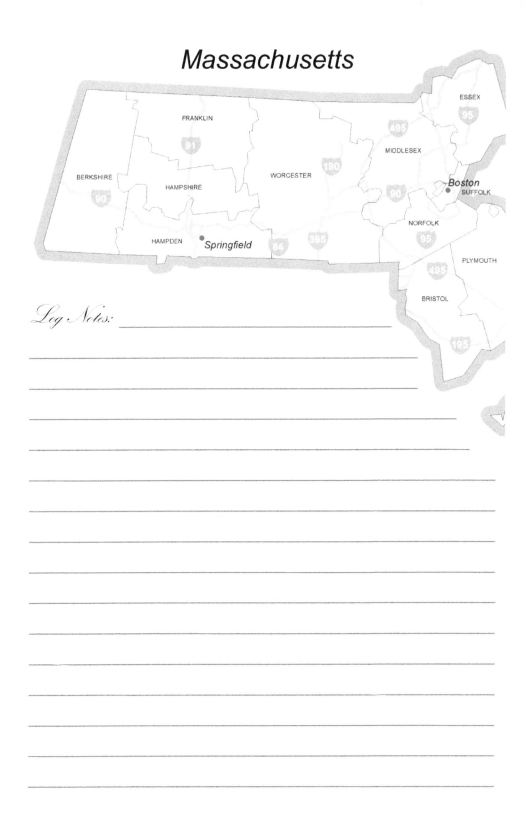

Log Notes:

Michigan

Log Notes:

Minnesota

Log Notes:

Mississippi

Log Notes:

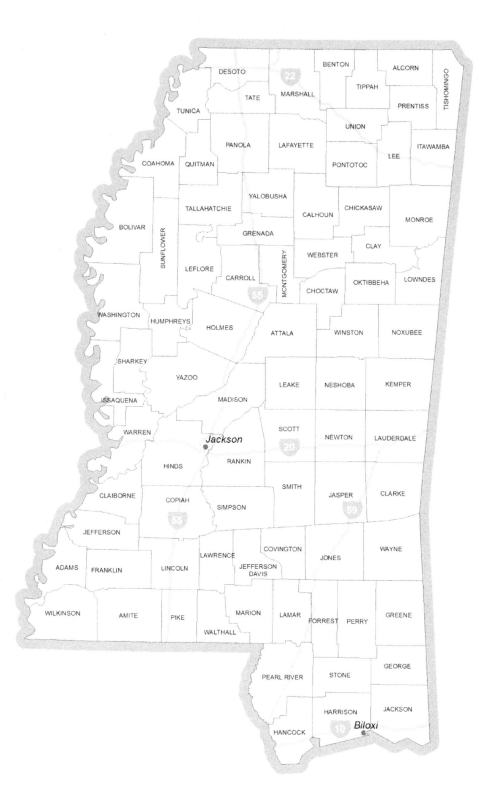

Missouri

Log Notes:

Montana

Log Notes:

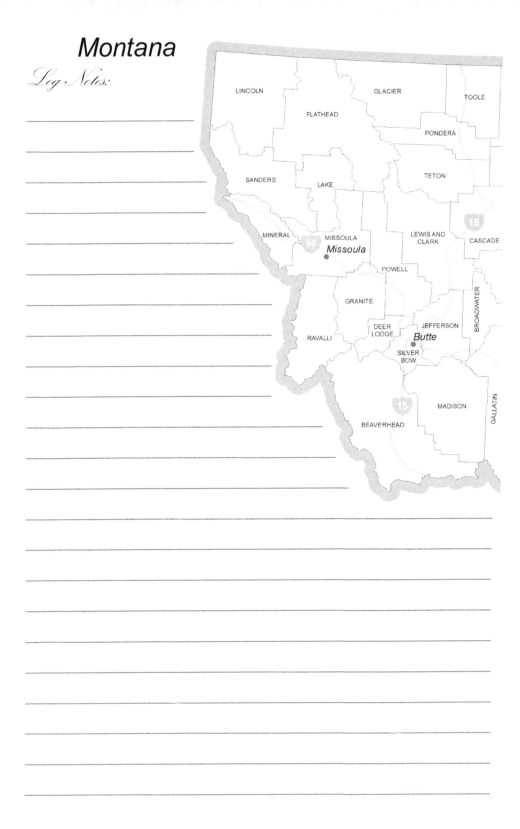

Nebraska

Log Notes: _____

_____
_____
_____
_____
_____
_____
_____
_____
_____
_____
_____
_____
_____
_____

Nevada

Log Notes: _____

_____
_____
_____
_____
_____
_____
_____
_____
_____
_____

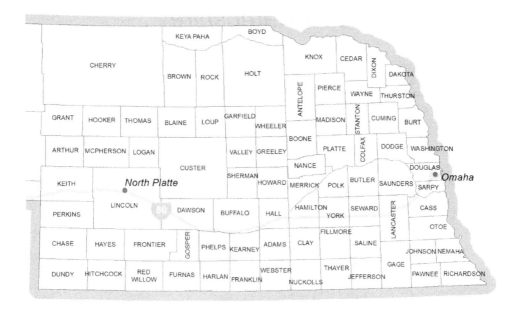

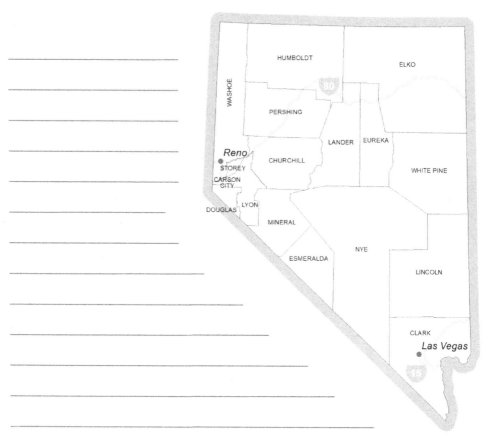

New Hampshire

Log Notes:

New Jersey

Log Notes:

New Mexico

Log Notes:

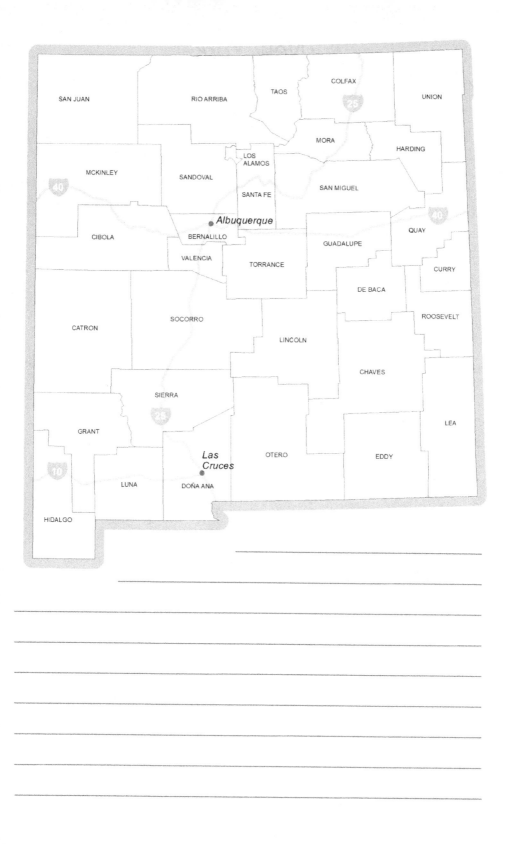

New York

Log Notes: _____

Log Notes:

North Dakota

Log Notes:

North Carolina

Log Notes:

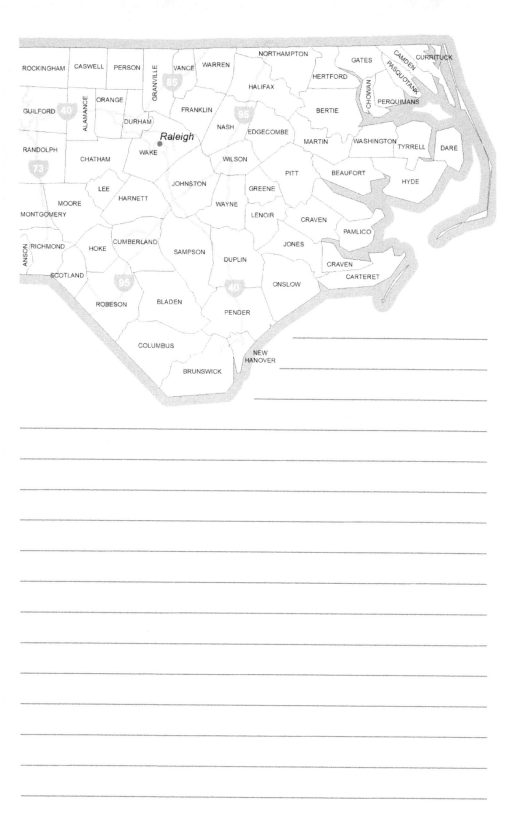

Ohio

Log Notes:

Oklahoma

Log Notes:

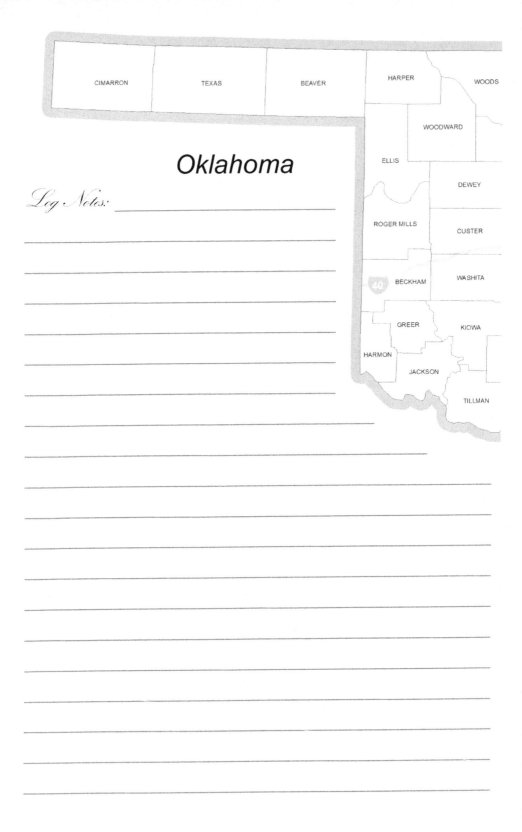

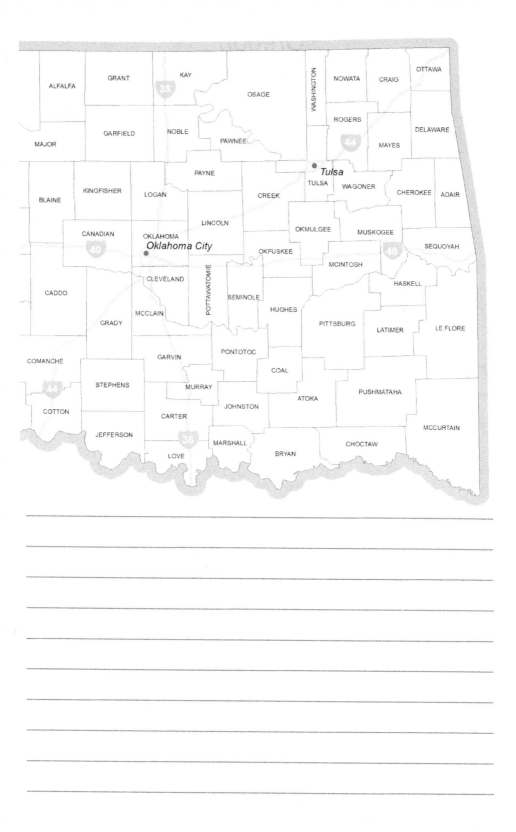

Oregon

Log Notes:

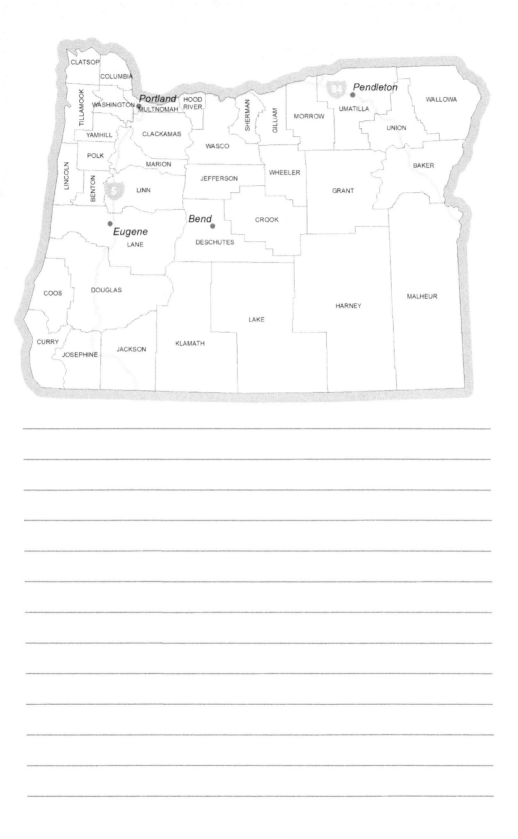

Pennsylvania

Log Notes:

Rhode Island

Log Notes:

South Carolina

Log Notes:

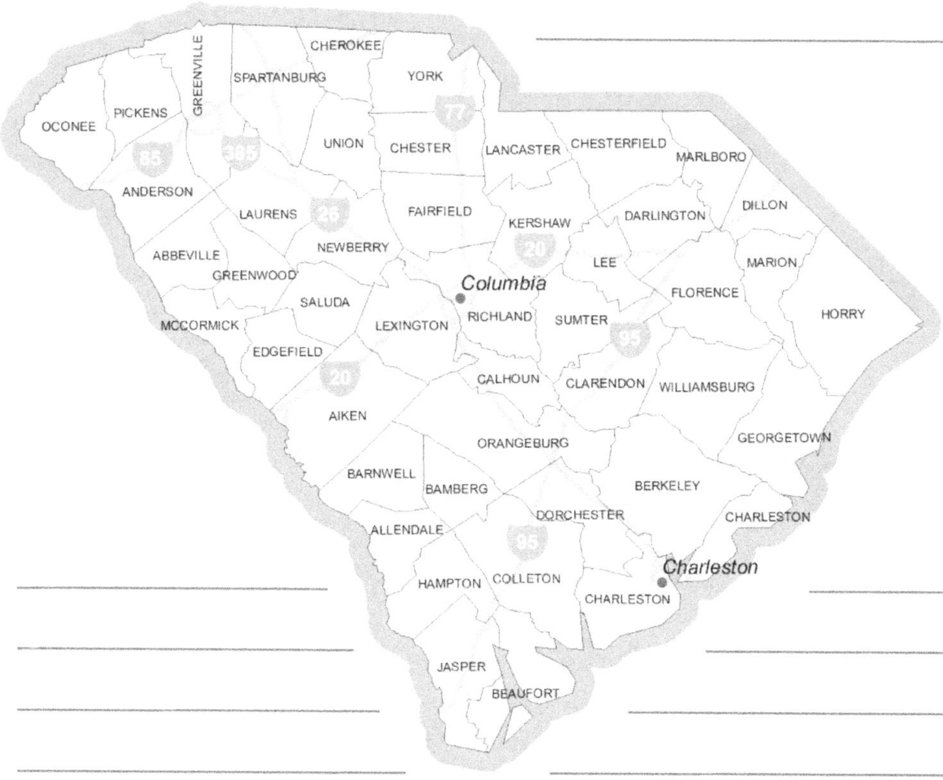

Log Notes:

South Dakota

Log Notes:

Tennessee

Log Notes:

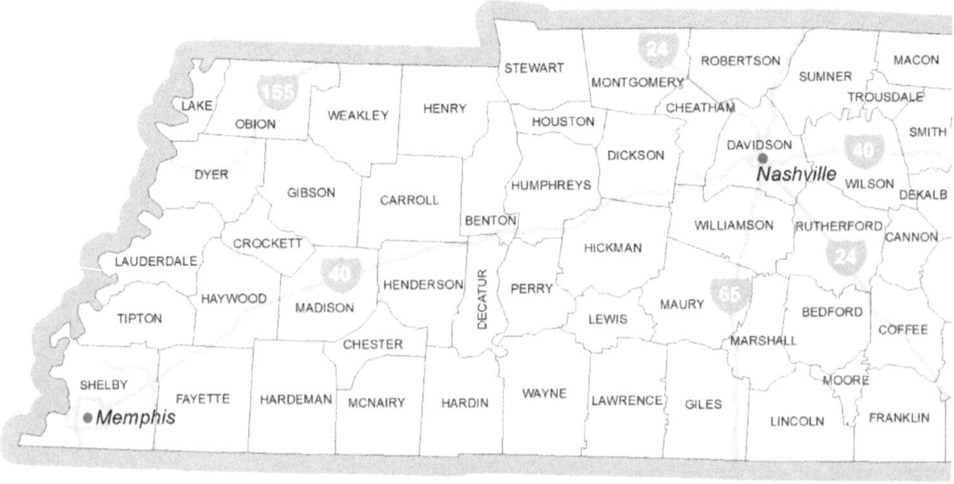

Texas

Log Notes:

Log Notes:

Utah

Log Notes: _____

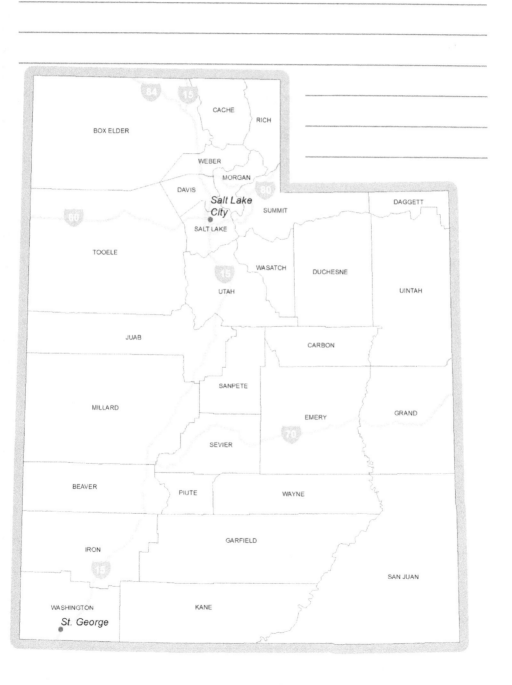

Log Notes:

Vermont

Log Notes:

Virginia

Log Notes:

Washington

Log Notes: _____

West Virginia

Log Notes:

Wisconsin

Log Notes:

Wyoming

Log Notes:

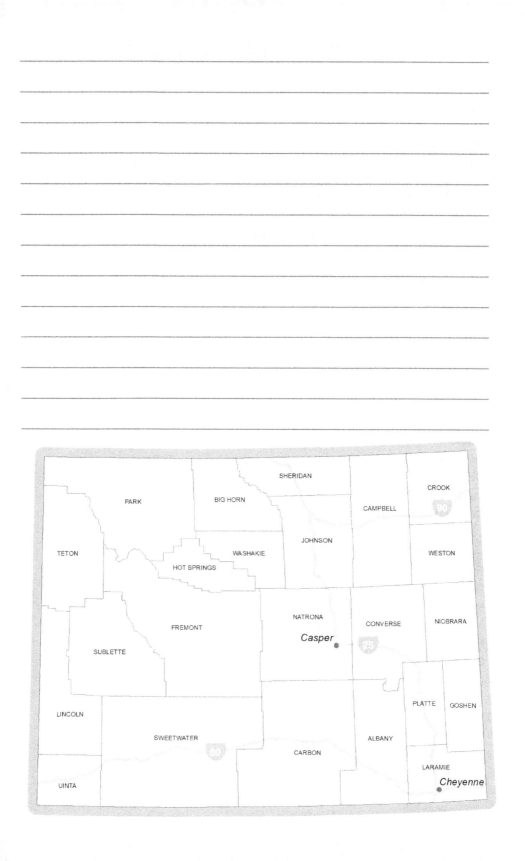

Countries of the World

North America
- ☐ Canada
- ☐ Mexico
- ☐ St. Pierre-Miquelon (FR)
- ☐ United States

Central America
- ☐ Belize
- ☐ Costa Rica
- ☐ El Salvador
- ☐ Guatemala
- ☐ Honduras
- ☐ Nicaragua
- ☐ Panama

Caribbean
- ☐ Anguilla (UK)
- ☐ Antigua & Barbuda
- ☐ Aruba (NL)
- ☐ Bahamas
- ☐ Barbados
- ☐ Bonaire (NL)
- ☐ Cayman Islands (UK)
- ☐ Cuba
- ☐ Curaçao (NL)
- ☐ Dominica
- ☐ Dominican Republic
- ☐ Grenada
- ☐ Guadeloupe (FR)
- ☐ Haiti
- ☐ Montserrat (UK)
- ☐ Martinique (FR)
- ☐ Sint Maarten (NL)
- ☐ St Kitts & Nevis
- ☐ St Lucia
- ☐ St Martin (FR)
- ☐ St Vincent & Grenadines
- ☐ Trinidad & Tobago
- ☐ Turks & Caicos (UK)
- ☐ Virgin Islands (UK)
- ☐ Virgin Islands (US)

South America
- ☐ Argentina
- ☐ Bolivia
- ☐ Brazil
- ☐ Chile
- ☐ Colombia
- ☐ Easter Island (CL)
- ☐ Ecuador
- ☐ Falkland Islands (UK)
- ☐ French Guiana (FR)
- ☐ Guyana
- ☐ Paraguay
- ☐ Peru
- ☐ Surinam
- ☐ Uruguay
- ☐ Venezuela

Europe
- ☐ Albania
- ☐ Andorra
- ☐ Austria
- ☐ Belarus
- ☐ Belgium
- ☐ Bermuda
- ☐ Bosnia-Herzegovina
- ☐ Bulgaria
- ☐ Croatia
- ☐ Czechia
- ☐ Denmark
- ☐ Estonia
- ☐ Finland
- ☐ France
- ☐ Germany
- ☐ Gibraltar (UK)
- ☐ Greece
- ☐ Greenland (DK)
- ☐ Holy See (Vatican)
- ☐ Hungary
- ☐ Iceland
- ☐ Ireland
- ☐ Italy
- ☐ Kosovo
- ☐ Latvia
- ☐ Liechtenstein
- ☐ Lithuania
- ☐ Luxembourg
- ☐ Malta
- ☐ Moldova
- ☐ Monaco
- ☐ Montenegro
- ☐ Netherlands
- ☐ North Macedonia
- ☐ Norway
- ☐ Poland
- ☐ Portugal
- ☐ Romania
- ☐ Russia
- ☐ San Marino
- ☐ Serbia
- ☐ Slovakia
- ☐ Slovenia
- ☐ Spain
- ☐ Sweden
- ☐ Switzerland
- ☐ Ukraine
- ☐ United Kingdom

Asia
- ☐ Afghanistan
- ☐ Armenia
- ☐ Azerbaijan
- ☐ Bahrain
- ☐ Bangladesh
- ☐ Bhutan
- ☐ Brunei
- ☐ Cambodia
- ☐ China
- ☐ Cyprus
- ☐ Georgia
- ☐ India
- ☐ Indonesia

- ☐ Iran
- ☐ Israel
- ☐ Japan
- ☐ Jordan
- ☐ Kazakhstan
- ☐ Kuwait
- ☐ Kyrgyzstan
- ☐ Laos
- ☐ Lebanon
- ☐ Malaysia
- ☐ Maldives
- ☐ Mongolia
- ☐ Myanmar
- ☐ Nepal
- ☐ North Korea
- ☐ Oman
- ☐ Pakistan
- ☐ Philippines
- ☐ Palestine
- ☐ Saudi Arabia
- ☐ Singapore
- ☐ South Korea
- ☐ Sri Lanka
- ☐ Syria
- ☐ Taiwan
- ☐ Tajikistan
- ☐ Thailand
- ☐ Timor-Leste
- ☐ Turkmenistan
- ☐ United Arab Emirates
- ☐ Uzbekistan
- ☐ Vietnam
- ☐ Yemen

Africa
- ☐ Algeria
- ☐ Angola
- ☐ Benin
- ☐ Botswana
- ☐ Burkina Faso
- ☐ Burundi
- ☐ Cape Verde
- ☐ Cameroon
- ☐ Canary Islands (SP)
- ☐ Central African Republic
- ☐ Chad
- ☐ Comoros
- ☐ Congo
- ☐ Djibouti
- ☐ Dem Rep Congo
- ☐ Egypt
- ☐ Equatorial Guinea
- ☐ Eritrea
- ☐ Eswatini
- ☐ Ethiopia
- ☐ Gabon
- ☐ Gambia
- ☐ Ghana
- ☐ Guinea
- ☐ Guinea-Bissau
- ☐ Kenya
- ☐ Lesotho
- ☐ Liberia
- ☐ Libya
- ☐ Madagascar
- ☐ Malawi
- ☐ Mali
- ☐ Mauritania
- ☐ Mauritius
- ☐ Mayotte
- ☐ Morocco
- ☐ Mozambique
- ☐ Namibia
- ☐ Niger
- ☐ Nigeria
- ☐ Réunion (FR)
- ☐ Rwanda
- ☐ Sao Tome & Principe
- ☐ Senegal
- ☐ Seychelles
- ☐ Sierra Leone
- ☐ Somalia
- ☐ South Africa
- ☐ South Sudan
- ☐ St Helena (UK)
- ☐ Sudan
- ☐ Tanzania
- ☐ Togo
- ☐ Tunisia
- ☐ Uganda
- ☐ Western Sahara
- ☐ Zambia
- ☐ Zimbabwe

Pacific/Other
- ☐ Antarctica (many)
- ☐ Australia
- ☐ Cook Island (NZ)
- ☐ Fiji
- ☐ French Polynesia (FR)
- ☐ Guam (US)
- ☐ Howland- Baker Is (US)
- ☐ Jarvis Island (US)
- ☐ Johnston Atoll (US)
- ☐ Kiribati
- ☐ Line Group (KR)
- ☐ Marshall Islands
- ☐ Micronesia
- ☐ Nauru
- ☐ New Caledonia (FR)
- ☐ New Zealand
- ☐ Norfolk Islands (AU)
- ☐ N Mariana Islands (US)
- ☐ Niue (NZ)
- ☐ Palau
- ☐ Palmyra Atoll (US)
- ☐ Papua New Guinea
- ☐ Phoenix Group (KR)
- ☐ Samoa
- ☐ Samoa (US)
- ☐ Solomon Islands
- ☐ Tokelau (NZ)
- ☐ Tonga
- ☐ Tuvalu
- ☐ Vanuatu
- ☐ Wake Island
- ☐ Wallis & Futuna (FR)

US National Park System

National Parks
- Acadia
- American Samoa
- Arches
- Badlands
- Big Bend
- Biscayne
- Black Canyon
- Bryce Canyon
- Canyonlands
- Capitol Reef
- Carlsbad Caverns
- Channel Islands
- Congaree
- Crater Lake
- Cuyahoga Valley
- Death Valley
- Denali
- Dry Tortugas
- Everglades
- Gates of the Arctic
- Gateway Arch
- Glacier
- Glacier Bay
- Grand Canyon
- Grand Teton
- Great Basin
- Great Sand Dunes
- Great Smoky Mtns
- Guadalupe Mtns
- Haleakalā
- Hawai'i Volcanoes
- Hot Springs
- Indiana Dunes
- Isle Royale
- Joshua Tree
- Katmai
- Kenai Fjords
- Kings Canyon
- Kobuk Valley
- Lake Clark
- Lassen Volcanic
- Mammoth Cave
- Mesa Verde
- Mount Rainier
- New River Gorge
- North Cascades
- Olympic
- Petrified Forest
- Pinnacles
- Redwood
- Rocky Mountain
- Saguaro
- Shenandoah
- Theodore Roosevelt
- Virgin Islands
- Voyageurs
- White Sands
- Wind Cave
- Wrangell–St. Elias
- Yellowstone
- Yosemite
- Zion

Historical Parks
- Abraham Lincoln Birthplace
- Adams
- Allegheny Portage
- Amache
- Andersonville
- Andrew Johnson
- Appomattox
- Bent's Old Fort
- Blackstone River
- Boston
- Boston African American
- Brown v. Board
- Cane River Creole
- Carl Sandburg Home
- Carter G. Woodson
- Cedar Creek & Belle Grove
- Chaco Culture
- Charles Pinckney
- Chesapeake & Ohio
- Christiansted
- Clara Barton
- Colonial
- Cumberland Gap
- Dayton Aviation
- Edgar Allen Poe
- Eisenhower
- Eleanor Roosevelt
- Eugene O'Neill
- First Ladies
- First State
- Ford's Theatre
- Fort Bowie
- Fort Davis
- Fort Laramie
- Fort Larned
- Fort Point
- Fort Raleigh
- Fort Scott
- Fort Smith
- Fort Sumter and Fort Moultrie
- Fort Union Trading Post
- Fort Vancouver
- Frederick Douglass
- Frederick L Olmsted
- Friendship Hill
- George Rogers Clark
- Golden Spike
- Grant-Kohrs Ranch
- Hampton
- Harpers Ferry
- Harriet Tubman
- Harriet Tubman Underground RR
- Harry S Truman
- Herbert Hoover
- Home of Franklin D. Roosevelt
- Homestead
- Honouliuli
- Hopewell Culture
- Hopewell Furnace
- Hubbell Trading Post
- Independence
- James A. Garfield
- Jean Lafitte
- Jimmy Carter
- John F Kennedy
- John Muir
- Kalaupapa
- Kaloko-Honokohau
- Keweenaw
- Klondike Gold Rush
- Knife River Villages
- Lewis and Clark
- Lincoln Home
- Little Rock Central High School
- Longfellow House
- Lowell
- Lyndon B. Johnson
- Maggie L. Walker
- Manhattan Project
- Manzanar
- Marsh-Billings-Rockefeller
- Martin L King, Jr.
- Martin Van Buren
- Mary Bethune Council House
- Minidoka
- Minute Man
- Minuteman Missile
- Morristown
- Natchez
- New Bedford Whaling
- New Orleans Jazz
- Nez Perce
- Nicodemus
- Ninety Six
- Ocmulgee Mounds
- Palo Alto Battlefield
- Paterson Great Falls
- Pecos
- Pennsylvania Avenue
- President Clinton Birthplace Home
- Pu'uhonua Honaunau
- Puukohola Heiau
- Rosie the Riveter
- Sagamore Hill
- Saint-Gaudens
- Saint Croix Island
- Saint Paul's Church
- Salem Maritime
- Salt River Bay
- San Antonio Missions
- San Francisco Maritime
- San Juan
- San Juan Island
- Sand Creek
- Saratoga
- Saugus Iron Works
- Sitka
- Springfield Armory
- Ste. Geneviève
- Steamtown
- Theodore Roosevelt Birthplace
- Theodore Roosevelt Inaugural
- Thomas Edison
- Thomas Stone
- Tumacacori
- Tuskegee Airmen
- Tuskegee Institute
- Ulysses S. Grant
- Valley Forge
- War in the Pacific
- Washita Battlefield
- Weir Farm
- Whitman Mission
- William Howard Taft
- Women's Rights

National Monuments
- African Burial Ground
- Agate Fossil Beds
- Alibates Quarries
- Aniakchak
- Aztec Ruins
- Bandelier
- Belmont-Paul
- Birmingham Civil Rights
- Booker Washington
- Buck Island Reef
- Cabrillo
- Camp Nelson
- Canyon de Chelly
- Cape Krusenstern
- Capulin Volcano
- Casa Grande Ruins
- Castillo de San Marcos
- Castle Clinton
- Castle Mountains
- Cedar Breaks
- César E. Chávez
- Charles Young Buffalo Soldiers
- Chiricahua
- Colorado
- Craters of the Moon
- Dinosaur
- Devils Tower
- Effigy Mounds
- El Malpais
- El Morro

☐ Florissant Fossil
☐ Fort Frederica
☐ Fort Matanzas
☐ Fort McHenry
☐ Fort Monroe
☐ Fort Pulaski
☐ Fort Stanwix
☐ Fort Union
☐ Fossil Butte
☐ George Washington Birthplace
☐ George Washington Carver
☐ Gila Cliff Dwellings
☐ Governors Island
☐ Grand Portage
☐ Hagerman Fossil
☐ Hohokam Pima
☐ Hovenweep
☐ Jewel Cave
☐ John Day Fossil Beds
☐ Katahdin Woods and Waters
☐ Lava Beds
☐ Little Bighorn
☐ Shenandoah
☐ Medgar and Myrlie Evers Home
☐ Mill Springs
☐ Montezuma Castle
☐ Muir Woods
☐ Natural Bridges
☐ Navajo
☐ Oregon Caves
☐ Organ Pipe Cactus
☐ Petroglyph
☐ Pipe Spring
☐ Pipestone
☐ Poverty Point
☐ Pullman
☐ Rainbow Bridge
☐ Russell Cave
☐ Salinas Pueblo
☐ Scotts Bluff
☐ Statue of Liberty
☐ Stonewall
☐ Sunset Crater
☐ Timpanogos Cave
☐ Tonto
☐ Tule Lake
☐ Tule Springs Fossil
☐ Tuzigoot
☐ Virgin Islands Coral Reef
☐ Waco Mammoth
☐ Walnut Canyon
☐ Wupatki
☐ Yucca House

National Memorials
☐ Arkansas Post
☐ Arlington House
☐ Chamizal
☐ Coronado
☐ De Soto
☐ Dwight Eisenhower
☐ Federal Hall
☐ Flight 93
☐ Fort Caroline
☐ Franklin D Roosevelt
☐ General Grant
☐ Hamilton Grange
☐ Johnstown Flood
☐ Lincoln
☐ Lincoln Boyhood
☐ Lyndon B Johnson Grove on Potomac
☐ Martin L King, Jr.
☐ Mount Rushmore
☐ Pearl Harbor
☐ Perry's Victory
☐ Port Chicago Naval
☐ Roger Williams
☐ Thadd. Kosciuszko
☐ Theodore Roosevelt Island
☐ Thomas Jefferson
☐ Vietnam Veterans
☐ Washington Monument
☐ World War I
☐ World War II
☐ Wright Brothers

Military Parks
☐ Antietam
☐ Big Hole
☐ Brices Cross Roads
☐ Chickamauga and Chattanooga
☐ Cowpens
☐ Fort Donelson
☐ Fort Necessity
☐ Fredericksburg & Spotsylvania
☐ Gettysburg
☐ Guilford Courthouse
☐ Horseshoe Bend
☐ Kennesaw Mountain
☐ Kings Mountain
☐ Manassas
☐ Monocacy
☐ Moores Creek
☐ Pea Ridge
☐ Petersburg
☐ Richmond
☐ River Raisin
☐ Shiloh
☐ Stones River
☐ Tupelo
☐ Vicksburg
☐ Wilson's Creek

Recreation Areas
☐ Amistad
☐ Bighorn Canyon
☐ Boston Harbor
☐ Chattahoochee River
☐ Chickasaw
☐ Curecanti
☐ Delaware Water Gap
☐ Gateway
☐ Gauley River
☐ Glen Canyon
☐ Golden Gate
☐ Lake Chelan
☐ Lake Mead
☐ Lake Meredith
☐ Lake Roosevelt
☐ Ross Lake
☐ Santa Monica Mtns
☐ Whiskeytown

National Shorelines
☐ Apostle Islands
☐ Assateague Island
☐ Canaveral
☐ Cape Cod
☐ Cape Hatteras
☐ Cape Lookout
☐ Cumberland Island
☐ Fire Island
☐ Gulf Islands
☐ Padre Island
☐ Pictured Rocks
☐ Point Reyes
☐ Sleeping Bear Dunes

National Rivers
☐ Alagnak
☐ Big South Fork
☐ Bluestone
☐ Buffalo
☐ Delaware
☐ Great Egg Harbor
☐ Mississippi
☐ Missouri
☐ Niobrara
☐ Obed
☐ Ozark
☐ Rio Grande
☐ Saint Croix
☐ Upper Delaware

National Preserves
☐ Bering Land Bridge
☐ Big Cypress
☐ Big Thicket
☐ Mojave
☐ Noatak
☐ Tallgrass Prairie
☐ Timucuan
☐ Valles Caldera
☐ Yukon-Charley Rivers

National Reserves
☐ City of Rocks
☐ Ebey's Landing
☐ Ice Age

National Reserves
☐ Big Thicket
☐ Mojave
☐ Noatak
☐ Tallgrass Prairie
☐ Timucuan
☐ Valles Caldera
☐ Yukon-Charley Rivers

National Trails
☐ Appalachian
☐ Potomac Heritage

National Parkways
☐ Blue Ridge
☐ George Washington
☐ John D. Rockefeller
☐ Natchez Trace

Other
☐ Capital Parks
☐ Catoctin Mountain
☐ Constitution Gardens
☐ Fort Washington
☐ Greenbelt
☐ National Mall
☐ Piscataway
☐ Prince William Forest
☐ Rock Creek
☐ White House
☐ Wolf Trap

Post August 2022
☐
☐
☐
☐
☐
☐
☐
☐
☐
☐

Made in United States
Orlando, FL
16 April 2024